YOUR PASSPORT TO

ECUADOR

Sarah Cords

raintree

a Capstone company — publishers for children

Raintree is an imprint of Capstone Global Library Limited, a company incorporated in England and Wales having its registered office at 264 Banbury Road, Oxford, OX2 7DY – Registered company number: 6695582

www.raintree.co.uk
myorders@raintree.co.uk

Edited by Jamie Hudalla
Designed by Colleen McLaren
Original illustrations © Capstone Global Library Limited 2021
Originated by Capstone Global Library Ltd
Printed and bound in India

978 1 3982 0545 1 (hardback)
978 1 3982 0546 8 (paperback)

British Library Cataloguing in Publication Data
A full catalogue record for this book is available from the British Library.

Acknowledgements
We would like to thank the following for permission to reproduce photographs: Alamy: Pere Rotger/Index/Heritage Image Partnership Ltd, 9; iStockphoto: 4FR, 16 (tortoise), Allan Watson, 21, DC_Colombia, cover (bottom); Newscom: Ballesteros/EFE, 12; Red Line Editorial: 5; Shutterstock Images: Abs Shrestha, 16 (seal), Agami Photo Agency, 16 (finch), Alejo Miranda, 19, betto rodrigues, 27, Brendan van Son, 6, Cao Romero, 22, Diego Grandi, 18, Ecuadorpostales, 11, Filip Bjorkman, cover (map), Fotos593, 15, Gil C, cover (flag), Guido Vermeulen-Perdaen, 16 (cormorant), Lukas Hodon, 28, Marek Poplawski, 7, Maridav, 16 (penguin), Neil Burton, 16 (iguana), nouseforname, 25, Ryan M. Bolton, 16 (lizard), Sidhe, 10, Terence Mendoza, 16 (locust)
Design Elements: iStockphoto, Shutterstock Images

We would like to thank Ernesto Capello, Professor of History and Latin American Studies at Macalester College, USA, for his assistance in the preparation of this book.

CONTENTS

Words in **bold** are in the glossary.

CHAPTER ONE

WELCOME TO ECUADOR!

The Pacific Ocean laps against the shore of the Galápagos Islands. Crabs and lizards crawl on the sandy beaches. A giant tortoise rests on a rock. These reptiles can weigh nearly 450 kilograms (1,000 pounds) and live to be 150 years old! Many people travel to the islands to see animals like these. The islands also have a variety of rare plants.

The islands belong to Ecuador, a country on the north-western coast of South America. People have lived on the land that is now Ecuador for thousands of years. Many cultures have shared the land. It was once a part of the **Inca Empire**. Spain also ruled the region.

MAP OF ECUADOR

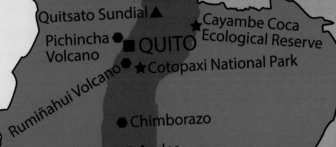

N
W E
S

- ■ Capital City
- ● City
- ⬡ Landform
- ▲ Landmark
- ★ Park

Quitsato Sundial ▲

Pichincha Volcano ⬡ ■ QUITO

★ Cayambe Coca Ecological Reserve

⬡ ★ Cotopaxi National Park

Rumiñahui Volcano ⬡

⬡ Chimborazo

⬡ Andes Mountains

● Guayaquil

Explore Ecuador's cities and landmarks.

Sea lions lie on the sandy beaches of the Galápagos Islands.

PEOPLE AND CLIMATE

More than 16 million people live in Ecuador. Some people work on farms, but most live in cities. More than 90 per cent of people speak Spanish. Others speak a **native** language called Kichwa.

Ecuador is on the equator. The equator is an invisible line that divides the Earth into its northern and southern **hemispheres**, or halves. Ecuador mainly experiences two seasons: wet and dry. The temperature is between 21 degrees Celsius (70 degrees Fahrenheit) and 27°C (80°F) all year. Because of the nice weather, people enjoy spending time in the beautiful natural areas. They also play outdoor sports such as football.

Some people in Ecuador live by the beach.

FACT FILE

OFFICIAL NAME: THE REPUBLIC OF ECUADOR
POPULATION: 16,498,502
LAND AREA: 276,841 SQ. KM (106,888 SQ. MI)
CAPITAL: QUITO
MONEY: US DOLLAR
GOVERNMENT: REPUBLIC, WITH AN ELECTED PRESIDENT
LANGUAGE: SPANISH AND KICHWA
GEOGRAPHY: Ecuador has different zones, including the Andes Mountains, tropical rainforests, beaches and the Galápagos Islands. Peru and Colombia border Ecuador.
NATURAL RESOURCES: Ecuador has bananas, oil, fish, crabs, lobsters and cocoa beans.

CHAPTER TWO

HISTORY OF ECUADOR

Different groups of people have lived in Ecuador over the years. One of the earliest peoples was the Valdivia. Some farmed and fished. Others made pottery bowls and jars.

The Valdivians lived in the area 5,500 years ago. They built their houses in a circle. The circle faced a public **plaza** where people could gather.

THE INCA EMPIRE

In the 1400s **CE**, Ecuador wasn't yet a country. Different groups of people split the area. In Cusco, a city in what is now Peru, the Inca Empire ruled. Around the year 1500, rulers of this empire moved into what is now Ecuador. People who already lived there fought against the empire. But the Inca won and took over the area.

Early groups of people in Ecuador made pottery figures.

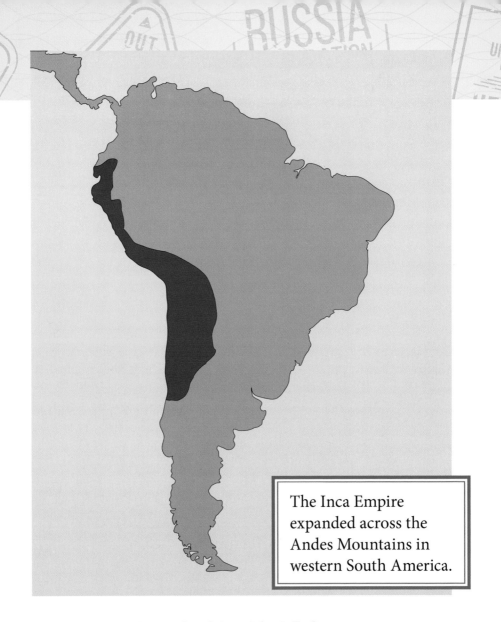

The Inca Empire expanded across the Andes Mountains in western South America.

SPANISH CONQUISTADORS

Soldiers from Spain, called **conquistadors**, arrived in Ecuador in the 1530s. An Inca leader, Atahualpa, and his men fought them but the Spanish killed him. Then one of Atahualpa's soldiers, Rumiñahui, fought the Spanish.

A volcano in Ecuador is named after Rumiñahui. The name means *rocky face.*

In 1534, Rumiñahui ordered the city of Quito to be destroyed. He wanted it gone so he wouldn't have to give it to the Spanish soldiers. The Spanish conquered the area. They began to rebuild Quito in 1534.

Before becoming president, Lenín Moreno was vice president from 2007–2013.

SPANISH COLONIAL RULE

Starting in the 1500s, Spain began colonizing parts of South America. From 1535 to 1822, Spain ruled Ecuador. Spain controlled Ecuador's money and treated the Spanish residents better than everyone else. The **indigenous** peoples of Ecuador grew frustrated with being treated so poorly. In 1809, rebels in Quito declared **independence** from Spain. They were the first people in South America to declare independence. In 1822, Ecuador became an independent country. Now the country is a **republic** with a president. Presidents can serve up to eight years in office.

ECUADOR'S PRESIDENT

The current head of state in Ecuador, President Lenín Moreno, was elected in 2017. He is one of the few world leaders to use a wheelchair.

CHAPTER THREE

EXPLORE ECUADOR

Ecuador is named after the equator. The equator runs through the middle of the planet. There are several sites to visit on the equator. One site is the Quitsato Sundial. It is a large instrument that tells time from the position of the Sun in the sky. When the Sun is directly overhead at noon, the sundial casts no shadow. People can also explore the Intiñan Solar Museum. Visitors go on tours and do science experiments set up by the museum. Many people also stop to take photographs by the Middle of the World monument. They can place one foot in the northern hemisphere and one foot in the southern hemisphere.

THE GALÁPAGOS ISLANDS

The Galápagos Islands are 1,000 kilometres (605 miles) off the coast of Ecuador. They consist of 13 major islands. They are a **UNESCO World Heritage Site**. These sites are important to everyone in the world.

Tourists can place one foot on each side of the equator at the Middle of the World monument.

ECUADOR 0°- 0'- 0" LAT.

RARE ANIMALS

BELOW ARE ANIMALS FOUND ONLY IN THE GALÁPAGOS ISLANDS

GALÁPAGOS TORTOISES

MARINE IGUANAS

LAVA LIZARDS

GALÁPAGOS FUR SEALS

GALÁPAGOS PENGUINS

FLIGHTLESS CORMORANTS

LARGE PAINTED LOCUSTS

DARWIN'S FINCHES

Some of the world's rarest animals, such as rainbow-coloured iguanas and blue-footed birds, live on the Galápagos Islands. One fish even looks like a bat!

MOUNTAINS AND VOLCANOES

In the centre of the country are the Andes Mountains. Two different ridges of this mountain range run side by side. The entire area is called the Andes Highlands, or the Sierra. Many volcanoes can be found here. This area is part of the Ring of Fire, an active trail of volcanoes along the Pacific Ocean.

FACT

There are more than 40 volcanoes in Ecuador and the Galápagos Islands. One volcano, Chimborazo, is the highest mountain in Ecuador. It is also the furthest distance on the planet from the centre of the Earth.

CENTURIES-OLD CITIES

Quito, Ecuador's capital, is a very old city. A famous section of the city is called Old Town. Many of its beautiful churches were built in the 1700s.

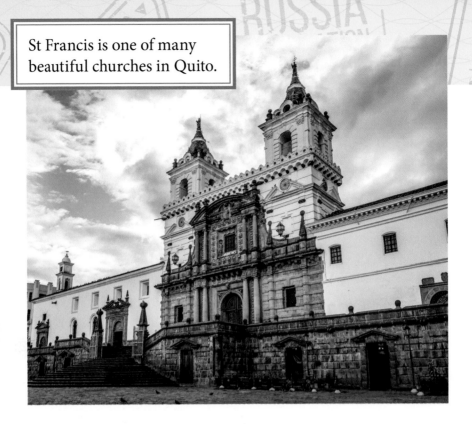

St Francis is one of many beautiful churches in Quito.

Quito is high in the Andes Mountains under the Pichincha volcano. More than 1.5 million people live there. It is a UNESCO World Heritage Site.

People pack the streets of Guayaquil, Ecuador's largest city. About 2.3 million people live there. Located on the country's southern coast, it is a major **port**. Most of Ecuador's **exports** are put on ships in Guayaquil. Then they are sent to the rest of the world. Visitors can discover history museums in Guayaquil. Presley Norton Museum contains items made by the ancient Valdivians.

Limpiopungo Lake and the volcano Cotopaxi are in Cotopaxi National Park.

BEAUTIFUL NATURAL AREAS

One of the most exciting parks in Ecuador is Cotopaxi National Park. It has an active volcano. Visitors walk and cycle in the park. People also enjoy the Cayambe Coca Ecological Reserve. This park has the tallest waterfall in Ecuador.

CHAPTER FOUR

DAILY LIFE

Family life is very important in Ecuador. Families host quinceañera parties to celebrate when girls turn 15. Young people often live with their parents even when they go to university. Family members, including grandparents and cousins, typically live near by.

MANY LANGUAGES

Most Ecuadorians speak Spanish. But that is not the only language spoken there. Another popular local language is Kichwa. Schools in Ecuador offer a **bilingual** education. They have classes in both Spanish and indigenous languages. Children in Ecuador usually start school around the age of six. University education is free.

FACT

In mountain communities, people often wear ponchos. Ponchos keep people warm and dry.

Several generations of a family often live together.

Plantain chips are often served as a side dish.

COMMON MEALS

Ecuador has many farms. Farmers grow crops such as plantain. A plantain is a type of banana that is usually cooked. Ecuador exports more bananas around the world than any other country!

PEOPLE OF ECUADOR

The majority of people who live in Ecuador are *mestizo*. They have both indigenous and European ancestors. Another group of people are known as the Montubio. They first lived on the coast of Ecuador. Other indigenous peoples include the Kichwa and the Shuar.

Various soups are popular in Ecuador. Soups are sometimes made using fish. They are often very spicy. Ecuadorians make empanadas, which are small meat pies. People also like llapingachos. These are pancakes made from mashed potatoes. They are often stuffed with cheese.

PLANTAIN CHIPS

About 10 per cent of the world's bananas are grown in Ecuador. That's about 6 million tonnes! People in Ecuador enjoy cooking one type of banana called a plantain. With the help of an adult, you can make plantain chips at home.

Ingredients:
- 4 plantains
- 3–4 tablespoons of olive oil
- Sea salt

Method:

1. Preheat oven to 200°C (400°F).
2. Peel plantains. Slice them very thinly.
3. Mix plantain slices with olive oil.
4. Cover an oven tray with tin foil and lay the slices on it.
5. Bake at 200°C for 17–20 minutes. They should be golden, but not too brown.
6. Take out of oven and let cool.
7. Lightly salt the slices.

CHAPTER FIVE

HOLIDAYS AND CELEBRATIONS

Some holidays in Ecuador are colourful displays of pride. The entire nation celebrates Independence Day on 10 August. That is the day the city of Quito declared independence from Spain in 1822. There are parades and fairs. People go to concerts. They enjoy traditional folk dances.

RELIGIOUS CELEBRATIONS

A lot of Ecuadorians follow the Roman Catholic religion. In the spring, they celebrate Easter. Before Easter, there is a time called Lent. It lasts for 40 days. During Lent, Catholics give up eating certain foods, such as meat. Before Lent is Carnival, usually in February or March. During Carnival, Ecuadorians march in parades. They throw coloured flour on each other. This activity stems from the indigenous practice of throwing flowers during celebrations.

Dancers put on performances during Carnival.

REGIONAL CELEBRATIONS

Many regions of Ecuador have their own holidays. At the end of August, the Yamor Festival is held in Otavalo. People celebrate farming and corn planting. There are parades. People dance and enjoy music. There is also a swimming race in nearby San Pablo Lake.

FACT

People celebrate Carnival with huge water balloon fights.

CHAPTER SIX

SPORT AND RECREATION

Football is very popular in Ecuador. There are 14 teams in its top national league. The Liga Deportiva Universitaria team from Quito played in the 2008 FIFA Club World Cup. They did not win, but they were the runners-up.

When athletes from Ecuador play games in Ecuador, they have a unique advantage. Ecuador is very mountainous. It is at high altitude. The air is thinner there than at low altitudes. Team members from other countries have to work harder just to breathe there. But athletes who are from Ecuador are used to the air. They don't get tired as quickly as their opponents.

Antonio Valencia is one of Ecuador's best footballers.

Ecuador is a good place to hike because it is a mountainous country.

A VARIETY OF ACTIVITIES

Another popular sport in Ecuador is paddle ball. The game is played with a soft ball. Players use paddles to hit the ball back and forth.

There are also many places for Ecuadorians to enjoy mountain climbing. Two mountain ranges in Ecuador contain high peaks. Visitors who climb these mountains have amazing views.

From fiery volcanoes to colourful cities, Ecuador has sites everyone can enjoy. Its warm weather and outdoor activities make it a great place to explore and live.

ECUAVOLEY

Ecuavoley is a sport similar to volleyball. The game is popular in Ecuador, especially in the city of Quito. Ecuadorians invented it in the late 1700s. To play, you will need six people, a football and a net.

1. Three players stand on each side of the net. Determine who will be the setter, the server and the flyer.
2. The server starts by throwing the ball over the net to the other team.
3. The setter and flyer take turns keeping the ball off the ground and hitting it to the other team. Teams score a point when the ball hits the ground on the other team's side.
4. A set consists of 15 points. The game is played until one team wins two sets.

GLOSSARY

bilingual
able to speak two languages

CE
CE means Common Era, or after year one

conquistadors
16th-century military leaders from Spain

export
sell and ship products to other countries

hemisphere
one half of Earth; the equator divides Earth into northern and southern hemispheres

Inca Empire
ruling empire in parts of Latin and South America, from the 1400s to 1532

independence
freedom a country has to govern itself

indigenous
first people, plants and animals to live in a country

native
born in a particular country or place; also, tied to a certain location

plaza
open area where people can gather

port
place where ships are loaded and unloaded

republic
type of government where people elect their political leaders and president

UNESCO World Heritage Site
landmark or area that is protected by an organisation called UNESCO. The sites are considered culturally, scientifically or historically important.

FIND OUT MORE

BOOKS

Galápagos Islands (In Focus), Clive Gifford (Kingfisher, 2018)

Geography Matters in the Inca Empire (Geography Matters in Ancient Civilizations), Melanie Waldron (Raintree, 2016)

Let's Look at Ecuador (Let's Look at Countries), Mary Boone (Raintree, 2020)

WEBSITES

kids.nationalgeographic.com/explore/countries/ecuador
Find out more about Ecuador with National Geographic.

www.bbc.co.uk/bitesize/topics/z3fycdm/articles/zk9cxyc
Explore the Galápagos Islands with BBC Bitesize.

www.dkfindout.com/uk/history/incas
DKfindout! gives you fun facts about the Incas.

INDEX

OTHER BOOKS IN THIS SERIES

YOUR PASSPORT TO CHINA

YOUR PASSPORT TO EL SALVADOR

YOUR PASSPORT TO ETHIOPIA

YOUR PASSPORT TO FRANCE

YOUR PASSPORT TO IRAN

YOUR PASSPORT TO KENYA

YOUR PASSPORT TO PERU

YOUR PASSPORT TO RUSSIA

YOUR PASSPORT TO SPAIN